RED MEAT

from the secret files of

Max Cannon

RED MEAT

a collection of RED MEAT cartoons

from the secret files of

Max Cannon

Foreword by Bill Griffith

St. Martin's Griffin
New York

For Jennifer, who never had a doubt

Special thanks to everyone who contributed in ways known and unknown

 For information, address St. Martin's Press, 175 Fifth Avenue, New York, N.Y. 10010.

RED MEAT is available for weekly newspaper syndication. For information contact Max Cannon at P.O. Box 41115, Tucson, AZ 85717 or email: **meatbiz@redmeat.com**

Visit the official RED MEAT website at www.redmeat.com

ISBN 0-312-18302-X

First published in the United States by Black Spring Books

First St. Martin's Griffin Edition: January 1998

10 9 8 7 6 5 4 3 2 1

Max Cannon's dreamy, machine-perfect cartoons make you laugh not by tickling your funnybone, but by metaphorically gnawing at it. As macabre and disturbing as the RED MEAT strips are, they're still not (ugh) "horror comics." Cannon mines a different, infinitely more original genre—the "horribly comic." The restrained, repeated images resemble a dark version (make that a very dark) of the familiar "What's wrong with this picture?" kids game. But, once we're lured in, Cannon (and his bolo-wearing crypt keeper, Earl, a Charles Baudelaire look-alike) brings out the fright mask—his real intention finally revealed. The chills, though, go more than skin-deep. Like a brain-damaged cousin to David Lynch's uneasy films, RED MEAT takes delight in the quease and sleaze beneath the sterile, everyday surface. And, hey, aren't those our treasured cultural archetypes he's using as "bait"?

RED MEAT doesn't merely challenge politically correct taboos and sacred cows—it happily ignores them. It inhabits that place where compelling comics always dwell—its own private universe, operating by its own demented rules.

—Bill Griffith, creator of **ZIPPY THE PINHEAD**

RED MEAT
come on, at least it's better than american cheese
from the secret files of
max cannon
Quit lookin' at me.

RED MEAT
dusty gewgaws from yesteryear
from the secret files of
max cannon
C'mon boy.
Play dead!
I'm just kidding...
he really is dead.

RED MEAT
perfectly pointless perfidy
from the secret files of
max cannon
The loss of a beloved pet is a tragic thing. Still though, I can't help but wonder–is that all there is to a dead dog...is that all there is?

RED MEAT
the people's beloved comic strip por vida
from the secret files of
max cannon
My dog is not dead, he just smells bad. I'll give him a bath.
Bad dog.

RED MEAT
the comic strip that just "is"
from the secret files of
max cannon
Whenever I'm feeling down I try to think about individuals who are less fortunate than myself.
If that doesn't work, I'll usually go and stalk someone...just to make the voices go away.

RED MEAT
the only comic strip drawn with ectoplasm
from the secret files of
Max Cannon
Psst! Hey kid, y'know who I am? I'm Babe Ruth – one of baseball's all time legends. At least, that's who I used to be before I died.
Now, to pay for my sins in life, I'm doomed to walk the Earth for eternity as a nine pound sea anemone.
Are you really "The Babe?"
Sure kid...sure. Say, you got a smoke? I'd give my left nut for a smoke. If I still had a left nut...

RED MEAT
touch this comic strip...please
from the secret files of
Max Cannon
Twenty-two years on the force, and now they tell me I'm tired...that I drink too much. Well let me tell you mister, I've never missed a day of work. Not one day! I've worked my ass off for peanuts. Sure I take a drink now and then...I've earned it.
Hey Stacy, I know it's prob'ly not a good time, but me'n the boys'd like to say somethin' on behalf'a all of us.
Sure Mike, I guess you guys must have a lotta emotions to express right now.
Well, actually we were thinking that since you're not gonna be needing it...maybe we could have your grey filing cabinet.
Thank you, guys. I realize that this is just your way of disguising your feelings of remorse at my leaving you after all these years.
I suppose you won't mind if we take the chair too, willya?

RED MEAT
the comic strip that just won't let up
from the secret files of
Max Cannon
I can't believe it...I've been canned. Twenty-two years of risking my neck every day and this is the thanks I get? Sure, I take a drink now and then... and maybe I did shoot the wrong guy a couple of times, but damn it, I gave it a thousand percent.
Now that I got nothing but time on my hands, maybe I could finally marry my girl Bess and we could settle down in Phoenix like we always talked about. Sure, I'll buy a little liquor store...
I hate to be the one to tell you this Stacy, but, two weeks ago Bess and I went to Vegas and tied the knot. I guess she got tired of waitin' around for you to propose.
Heh! Y'know Mike, if I didn't know you were just ribbing me, I'd be inclined to blow your head clean off.
I mean it, Stacy. Now, let's have your gun and badge.

RED MEAT
hey kids...color this comic strip
from the secret files of
max cannon
Y'know Stacy, you been coming into my bar for twelve years and every time I see you you're down in the dumps. To hear you tell it, nothing ever goes your way. I mean, you gotta be the most depressing guy I ever met. Just once I'd like to hear something other than a complaint come outta your mouth...
Have it your way.
Nngk...BLEEEEEEAAAAAAAGH!!
Get out.
Wait...I think there's more.

RED MEAT
this week's comic strip is drawn by the lucky coloring contest winner: billy, age 8
from the secret files of
max cannon
My LiFe is A roTen BuMMer. I hope NoThing bad hapens.
oops. I have weT My panTs.
WET
At LeasT it is warM. WhaT a LUCKY Brake!

RED MEAT
my kid could draw a better comic strip
from the secret files of
max cannon
I AM BUMed. I WILL BY Sex FroM a prosiTuT.
LaTer...
Ah Now I aM feLing BeTTer.
oh no. CraBes!

RED MEAT
the comic strip that's not fooling anyone
from the secret files of
Max Cannon
≷Sigh≶ Sleeping in the park. I never thought it would come to this. What happened? Everyone I know has turned their back on me: my former colleagues at the police department, my best girl, even my favorite bartender...they all hate me. Y'know, sometimes I feel like the pigeons in this park are the only real friends I have left.
Wish I still had my gun.

RED MEAT
aren't you a little old to be reading comics?
from the secret files of Max Cannon
In the night, Stacy is visited by a dark stranger...
Stacy...get up.
Grrroooaaan...
Get a grip on yourself man. It doesn't look good for the rest of us if the public sees a...uh...retired crimefighter sleeping in the city park and reeking of spiritous liquor.
I-I just feel so down. I don't know what to do.
Well, I've always found that leotards make a big difference...not only in the way I look—but in the way that I feel, too.
Beat it, ya homo.

RED MEAT
your best insurance policy against accidental mirth
from the secret files of
max cannon
Stacy lies unmoving on a park bench. Paralyzed by depression, he cannot react to the world around him. For three weeks he has been in this terrible state...
Just then, a gentle rain begins to fall...
How fortunate. A gentle, cleansing rain... Hey, where's that awful smell coming from?
Regrettably, it is not rain–but the ammoniated urine from a freak swarm of bats that is passing overhead.
GAG! All creation mocks me.

RED MEAT
the comic stripped bare
from the secret files of
max cannon
Mornin' Mike. You scavenging pebbles for the egg chamber?
That's what the foreman tells me. And yourself?
Since you asked, I gotta go fertilize the queen.
Whoa! Nice work if you can get it.
Hey, this guy's deader'n a doornail.
Great! Let's eat.

RED MEAT
the comic strip where the bodies pile up like cordwood
from the secret files of
Max Cannon
Floating above the park bench, Stiff Stacy views his own body below him. He feels a strange calm take him as he floats weightlessly upward through a long blue tunnel toward a bright and unearthly light...
Overwhelmed by a profound sense of joy and warmth, he is soon rejoicing with departed loved ones. Stiff Stacy feels no regret as he leaves behind his former life.
But wait...it is only a short-lived illusion. Mercifully, this bitter realization fades as Stacy's awareness rapidly spirals into a dark and hopeless oblivion...
Hey Leo, I tell ya he's stiff as a board! Let's go put him on your girlfriend's porch swing.

RED MEAT
the comic strip of gratuitous mystery
from the secret files of
Max Cannon
Is it still there?

RED MEAT
the comic strip under your bed
from the secret files of
Max Cannon
Hey Chuck, guess how many fingers I have.
T-Ten?
Wrong. I have ten on my hands...but I have three more in my coat pocket!
MO-O-OM!! Choppo's scaring me!
Go to bed, Chuck.
Aha-ha-ha-ha.

RED MEAT
the comic that helps get your mind off the itching
from the secret files of
max cannon
STACY!! We thought you were dead!
Heh. It just so happens that I was *almost* dead. Fortunately, just as I was about to buy the farm, I was bitten repeatedly by a radioactive sewer roach.
The remarkable properties of the radioactive roach bacteria comingled with my bloodstream and a particular brand of inexpensive liquor (the name of which escapes me) caused a startling metamorphosis that brought me back to life, and imbued me with incredible superhuman abilities.
What kind of abilities?
So far, I can only run across the kitchen floor at tremendous speeds. However, I am thinking about getting a costume made.

RED MEAT
sweat gets in your eyes
from the secret files of
Max Cannon
Later, at police headquarters...
What's with the leotards, Stacy? You goin' trick or treating?
I am no longer Stiff Stacy. Just call me..."The Roach."
Ah-ha! ha! The Roach! Ah-ha! ha!
To better utilize my incredible superhuman abilities, I have donned this guise to strike fear into the hearts of the naturally superstitious criminal element.
When the crooks see you, they're sure to die laughing!
Did I mention that I now carry seven major infectious diseases?
Hey, back off, Stacy.

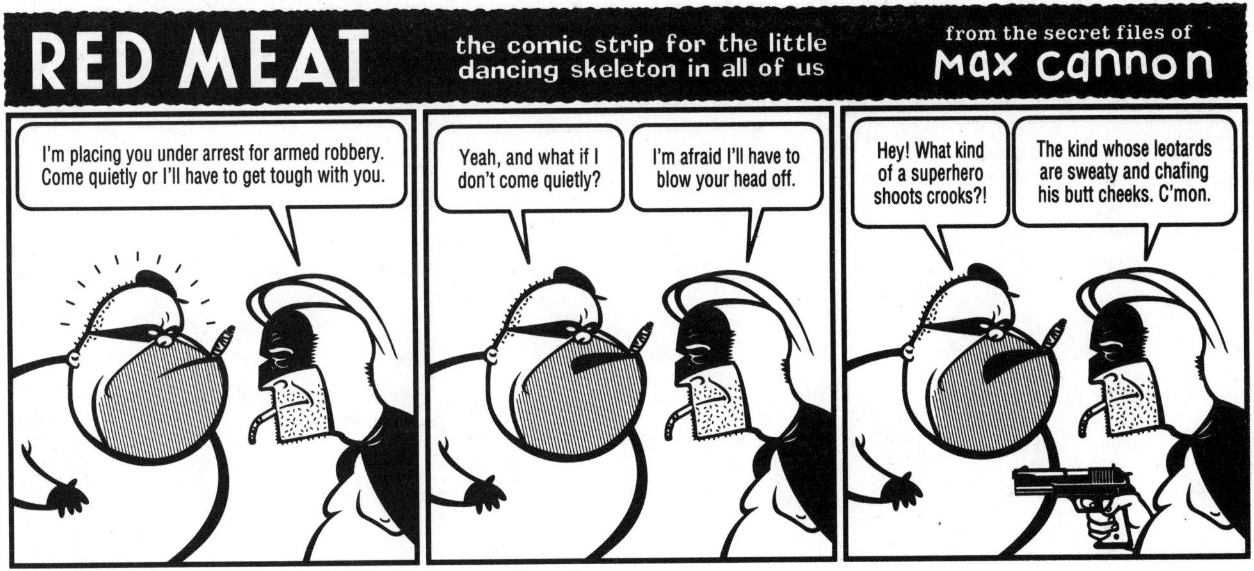
RED MEAT
the comic strip for the little dancing skeleton in all of us
from the secret files of
max cannon
I'm placing you under arrest for armed robbery. Come quietly or I'll have to get tough with you.
Yeah, and what if I don't come quietly?
I'm afraid I'll have to blow your head off.
Hey! What kind of a superhero shoots crooks?!
The kind whose leotards are sweaty and chafing his butt cheeks. C'mon.

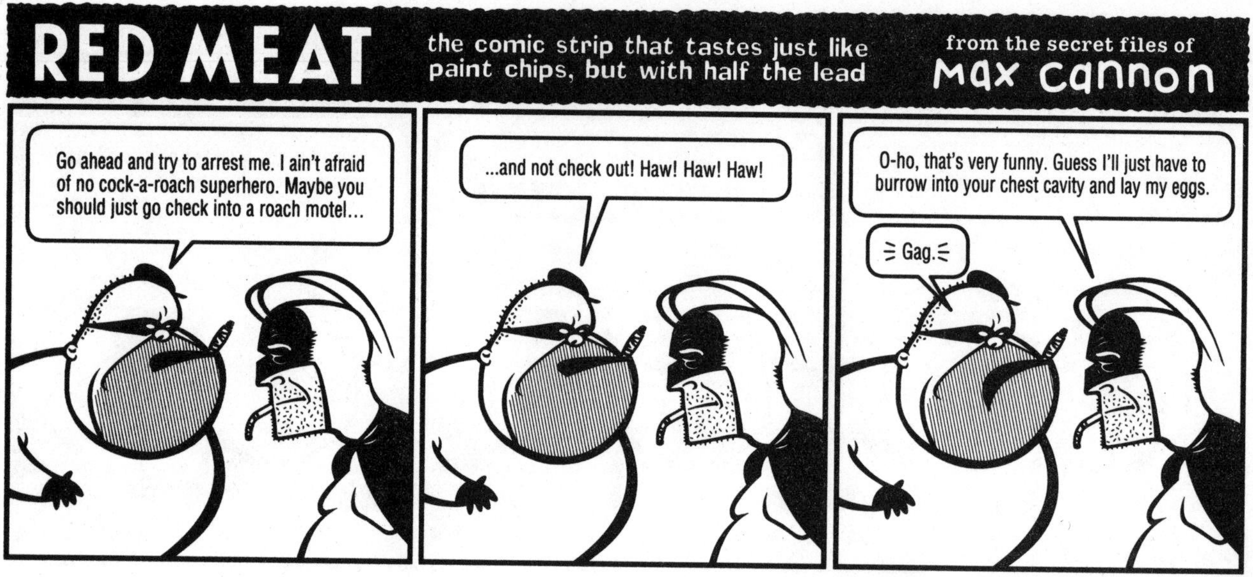
RED MEAT
the comic strip that tastes just like paint chips, but with half the lead
from the secret files of
Max Cannon
Go ahead and try to arrest me. I ain't afraid of no cock-a-roach superhero. Maybe you should just go check into a roach motel...
...and not check out! Haw! Haw! Haw!
O-ho, that's very funny. Guess I'll just have to burrow into your chest cavity and lay my eggs.
Gag.

RED MEAT
humor that snaps your funnybone
from the secret files of
max cannon
When I was workin' in the hospital, I seen this one room in the basement where there was all these sick little babies. They all had some kind of funny-lookin' gadgets hooked on their heads.
They also had all these tubes going into their arms and legs, and those tubes was hooked up to a big drum of some yellow stuff. Once a day, two guys wearing uniforms from that famous hamburger restaurant chain would come in and refill the drum.
Sometimes they would bring me french fries.

RED MEAT
constructed from an ancient method using wattle and pitch
from the secret files of
Max Cannon
A long time ago, my Brother and I found a dead clown in the desert in back of our parent's house.
It struck us as very unusual, since there had been no circus in town. We got two ping pong balls and drew circles on them with a black magic marker.
We put them on the clown's face. Then we laughed really hard at that clown, even though he was dead.

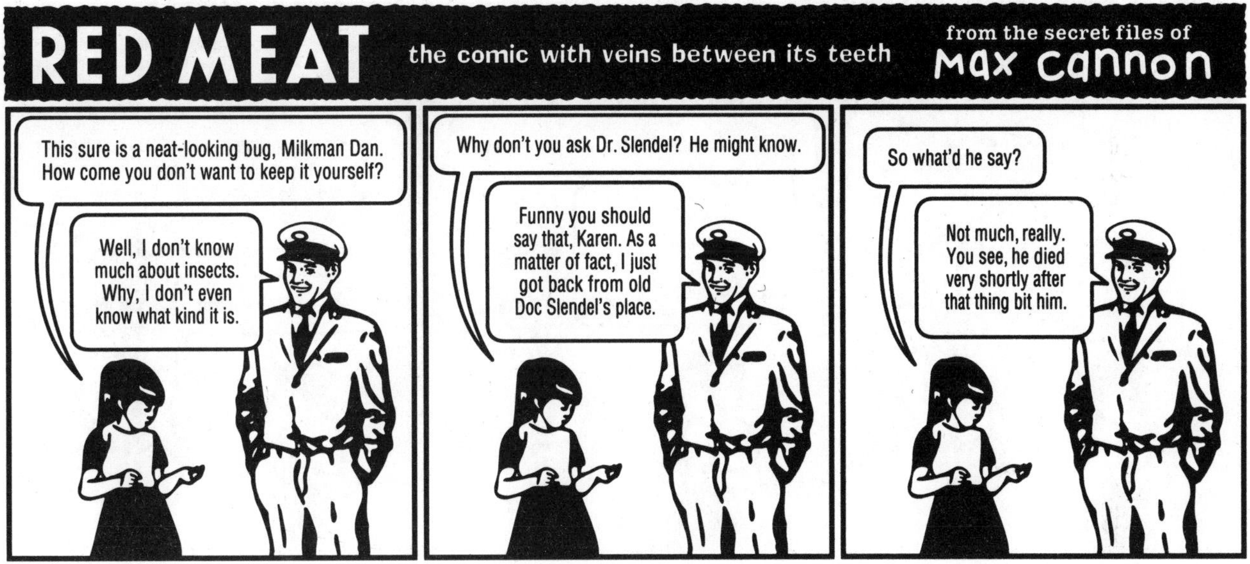
RED MEAT
the comic with veins between its teeth
from the secret files of
Max Cannon
This sure is a neat-looking bug, Milkman Dan. How come you don't want to keep it yourself?
Well, I don't know much about insects. Why, I don't even know what kind it is.
Why don't you ask Dr. Slendel? He might know.
Funny you should say that, Karen. As a matter of fact, I just got back from old Doc Slendel's place.
So what'd he say?
Not much, really. You see, he died very shortly after that thing bit him.

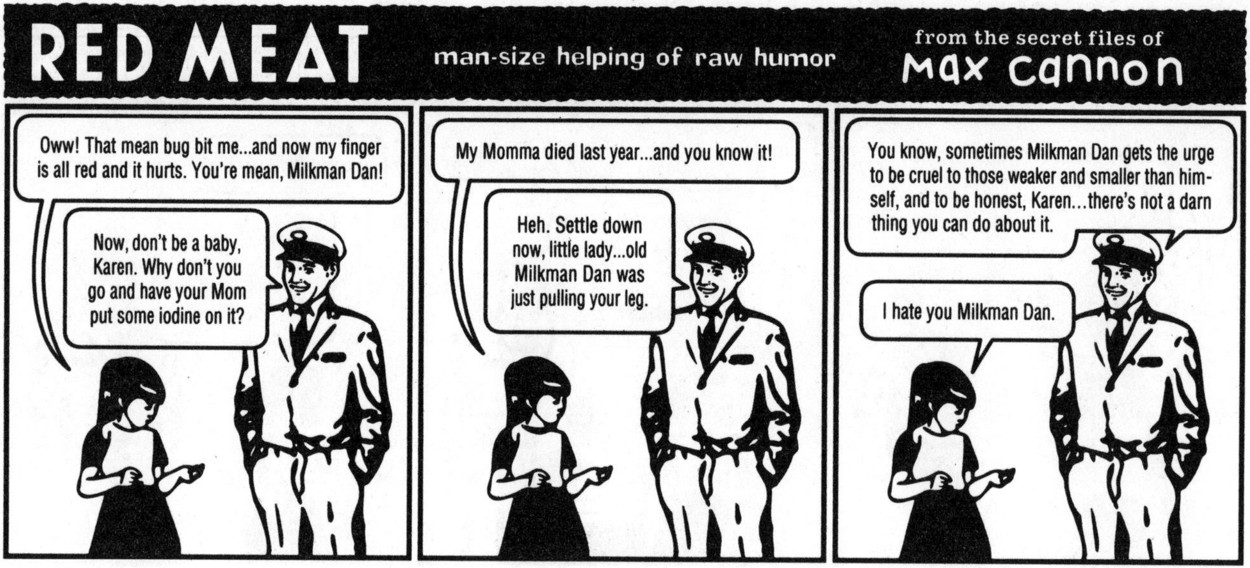
RED MEAT
man-size helping of raw humor
from the secret files of
max cannon
Oww! That mean bug bit me...and now my finger is all red and it hurts. You're mean, Milkman Dan!
Now, don't be a baby, Karen. Why don't you go and have your Mom put some iodine on it?
My Momma died last year...and you know it!
Heh. Settle down now, little lady...old Milkman Dan was just pulling your leg.
You know, sometimes Milkman Dan gets the urge to be cruel to those weaker and smaller than him-self, and to be honest, Karen...there's not a darn thing you can do about it.
I hate you Milkman Dan.

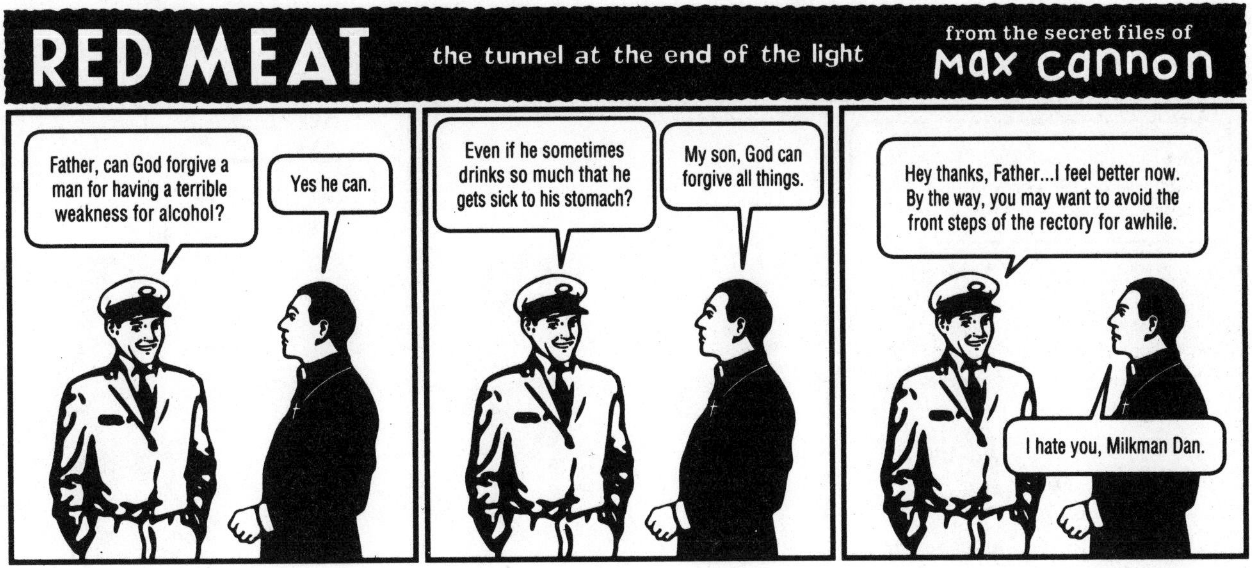
RED MEAT
the tunnel at the end of the light
from the secret files of
Max Cannon
Father, can God forgive a man for having a terrible weakness for alcohol?
Yes he can.
Even if he sometimes drinks so much that he gets sick to his stomach?
My son, God can forgive all things.
Hey thanks, Father...I feel better now. By the way, you may want to avoid the front steps of the rectory for awhile.
I hate you, Milkman Dan.

RED MEAT
a worse today for a better tomorrow
from the secret files of
max cannon
Lord, I pray that you will forgive Milkman Dan for his transgressions, and give him wisdom so that he may truly see the error of his ways.
Well, well. Aren't we "Little Mr. Perfect?"

RED MEAT
the comic strip that hasn't been the same since yoko joined the band
from the secret files of
max cannon
unnh...unh..uh.
unh...unnh...unh.
Beethoven's ninth month: first movement.

RED MEAT
Little bits of cartoon gristle for your chewing pleasure
from the secret files of
Max Cannon
Mmm...good ol' dang coffee! Boy howdy, I surely do love the cowboy life. A feller can do some fine livin' out here in the lonesome, wide open spaces.
Hell yes, the work's long and the pay's short. But out here a man always knows where he stands. I reckon this is the way the Lord intended for a man to live.
Whooeee! I feel s'dang good I think I'll have another cup a' coffee and take a coupla hits a' speed an' then go write my name on the side of a cow with my own pee.

RED MEAT
the hills are alive with the sound of meat
from the secret files of max cannon
About a week after we found that dead clown, my brother and I were up late flipping through the UHF dial to see if anything was still on. We only found one channel, and to our surprise, there was that clown.
The show was really strange. It seemed like a children's show, but there were no cartoons or games or anything. It was just that dumb clown waving a gun around and yelling stuff at a crappy-looking uncle sam puppet.
We thought it was a really boring show, but we watched it anyway, until my Dad came downstairs, turned off the TV, and told us to go to bed. The next morning we went to the place where we had put that dead clown under a tree and shot our bee-bee guns at him for a couple of hours.
POINK!

RED MEAT
the finish line for the human race
from the secret files of
Max Cannon
Oh, would you just look at this darling little Hummel figurine! Isn't it just precious? Oh Ted, I'm going to collect all of them!
BLAM!
Had to be done.

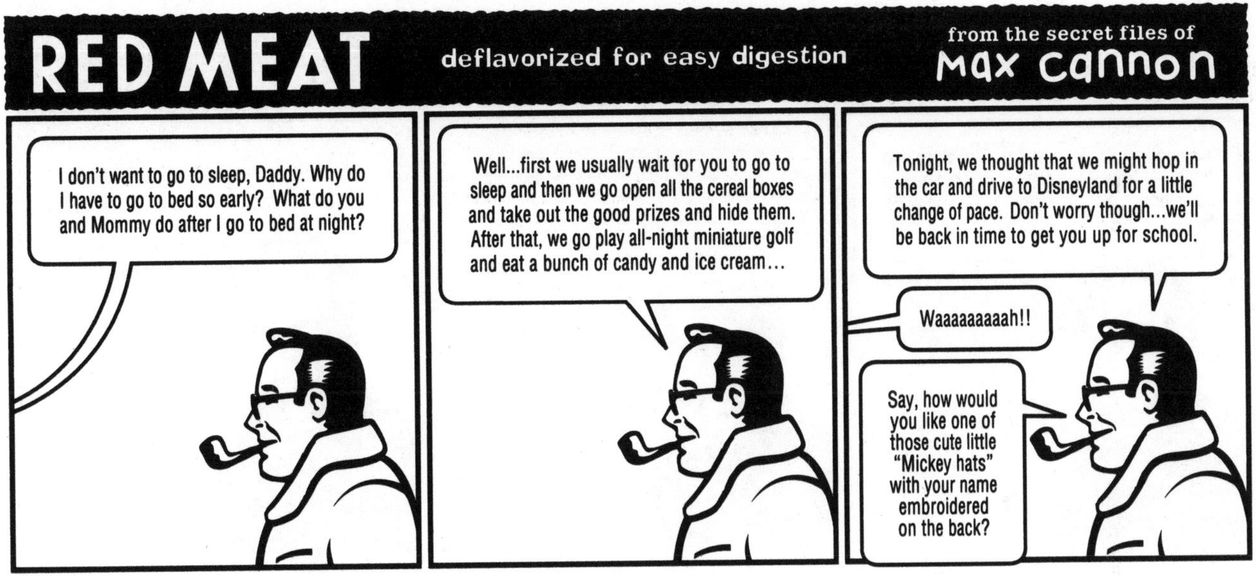
RED MEAT
deflavorized for easy digestion
from the secret files of
Max Cannon
I don't want to go to sleep, Daddy. Why do I have to go to bed so early? What do you and Mommy do after I go to bed at night?
Well...first we usually wait for you to go to sleep and then we go open all the cereal boxes and take out the good prizes and hide them. After that, we go play all-night miniature golf and eat a bunch of candy and ice cream...
Tonight, we thought that we might hop in the car and drive to Disneyland for a little change of pace. Don't worry though...we'll be back in time to get you up for school.
Waaaaaaaaah!!
Say, how would you like one of those cute little "Mickey hats" with your name embroidered on the back?

RED MEAT
in the company of misery
from the secret files of
max cannon
I seen Santy Claus the other night at the dog track, but he wasn't none too jolly cuz he was losin' pretty bad. Later on, when I was walkin' home, I hear this noise comin' from a dumpster.
I looked inside, and it was Old Saint Nick hisself... moanin' and holdin' onto his guts. He looked pretty worked over, and I seen enuff ta know he'd been roughed up by a couple of goons who were tryin' to collect on a "loan." Anyways, I wasn't lookin' for no trouble, so I just left him in there. Besides...
I never did get them roller skates I asked for.

RED MEAT
mondo turbid
from the secret files of
max cannon
Nnngh! Gnnngk!
Ungh...eeeeaaaaah!
So that's an enema...well, I'll be darned.

RED MEAT
the comic drill-bit for your cranium
from the secret files of
max cannon
Right now you're probably asking yourself: "Did he fire five shots...or six?" Well, to tell you the truth, in all this excitement I lost count. But seeing as this is the most powerful handgun in the world, there's one question you have to ask yourself...
MOST POWERFUL HANDGUN IN THE WORLD
If you're really interested mister, you fired two shots as I was walking across the yard, you got off one round when I ducked behind the mailbox, and three more as I dove for the porch. That'd be six shots.
However, seeing as how I'm packing a .38 caliber snub-nose that I purchased at Sport-n-Stuff for $69.95 (no questions asked) which I haven't fired yet, there's one question you have to ask yourself: "How many boxes of band candy am I gonna buy?"
You're okay, kid. Want a cold beer?
CHEAP, BUT EFFECTIVE HEATER

RED MEAT
in glorious black and white
from the secret files of
max cannon
What are you doing Ted? Get into your costume, or we're going to be late for the Halloween party!
I'm already wearing my costume, Sweetheart...
Can't you tell? I'm a naked burglar.
Why don't you just take off the mask—and your wedding ring—and go as a naked ex-husband?
But, Honey...I paid 79¢ for this mask.

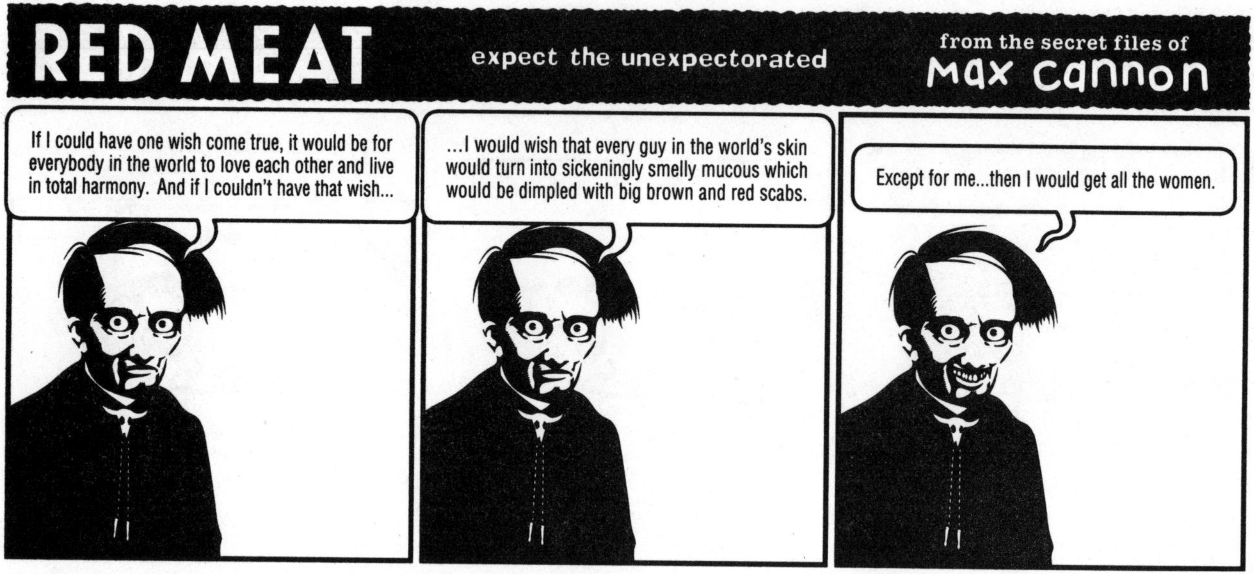
RED MEAT
expect the unexpectorated
from the secret files of
max cannon
If I could have one wish come true, it would be for everybody in the world to love each other and live in total harmony. And if I couldn't have that wish...
...I would wish that every guy in the world's skin would turn into sickeningly smelly mucous which would be dimpled with big brown and red scabs.
Except for me...then I would get all the women.

RED MEAT
the runny side of life
from the secret files of
max cannon
Ted, you've been out on the porch for hours. Why don't you come inside?
It's the damnedest thing, honey... the sky is clear as a bell, and yet there isn't a star in the sky at all.
Why don't you try going back out tonight when it gets dark. Maybe you'll see some stars then. Come in...your lunch is ready.
Hmmm...
Sweetheart...did you use cough syrup to flavor the cherry coffee cake again?
Of course I did. It's in the recipe, sillyhead!

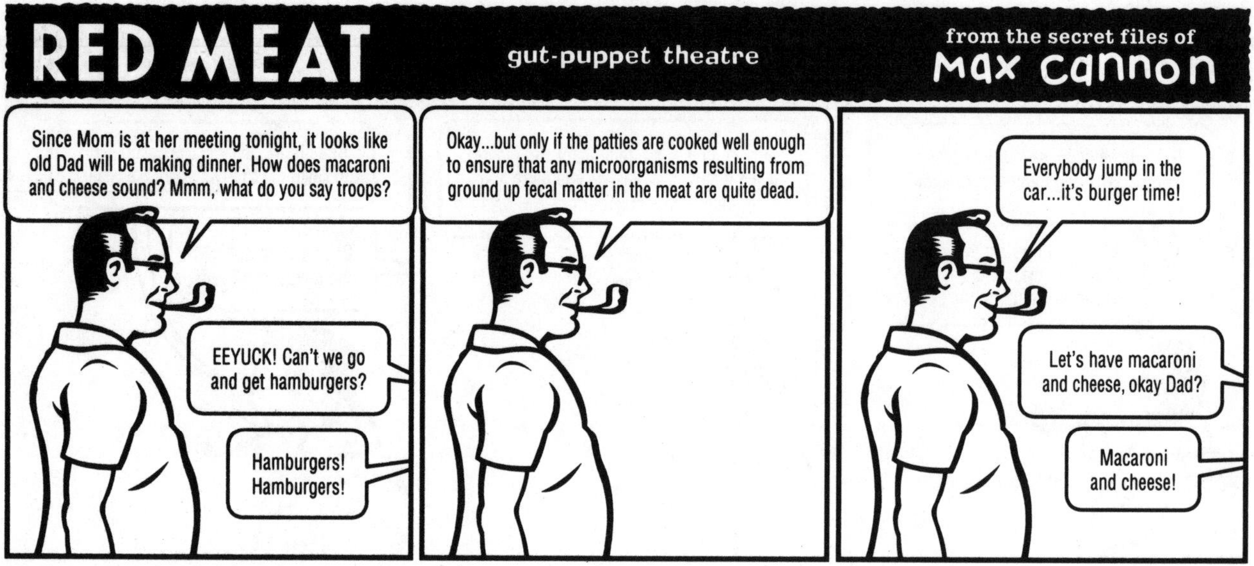
RED MEAT
gut-puppet theatre
from the secret files of
max cannon
Since Mom is at her meeting tonight, it looks like old Dad will be making dinner. How does macaroni and cheese sound? Mmm, what do you say troops?
EEYUCK! Can't we go and get hamburgers?
Hamburgers! Hamburgers!
Okay...but only if the patties are cooked well enough to ensure that any microorganisms resulting from ground up fecal matter in the meat are quite dead.
Everybody jump in the car...it's burger time!
Let's have macaroni and cheese, okay Dad?
Macaroni and cheese!

RED MEAT
abusement park
from the secret files of
Max Cannon
Gosh darn it all!!
Daddy wet his pants on the roller coaster! Daddy wet his pants on the roller coaster!
Okay, okay, so I wet my pants...
...but that's only half the story.

RED MEAT
humorous table-saw mishap
from the secret files of
Max Cannon
Father, I got a serious problem. Sometimes I like to go down to the gym and watch guys working out, and well, I kind of get...um, you know...excited by it.
Hmmm...I see.
Where exactly is this...gym?

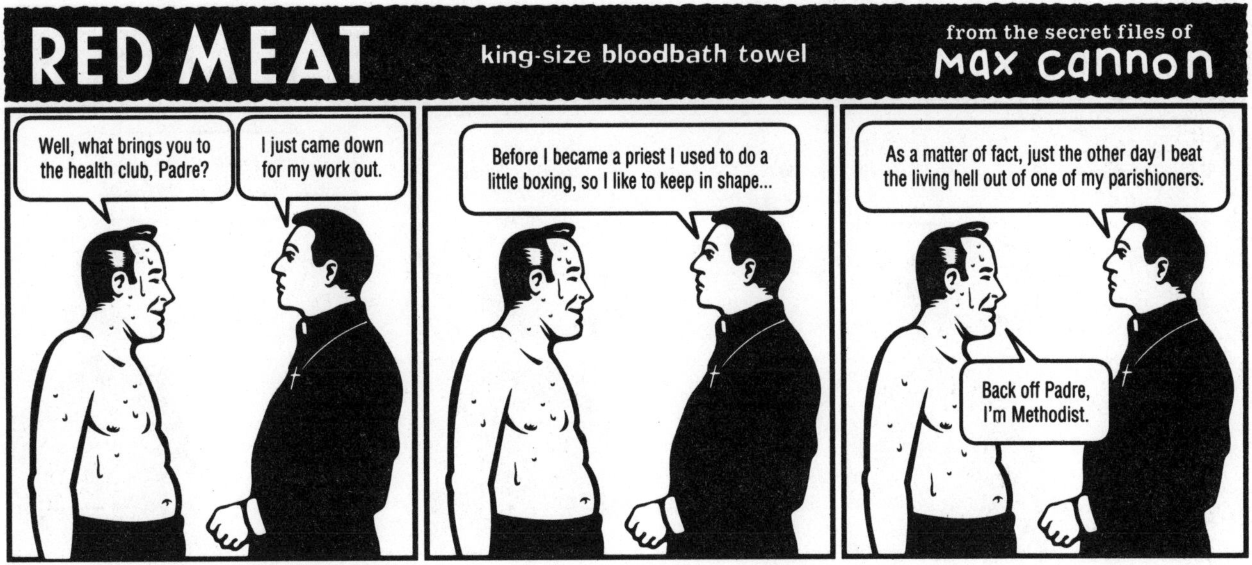
RED MEAT
king-size bloodbath towel
from the secret files of
max cannon
Well, what brings you to the health club, Padre?
I just came down for my work out.
Before I became a priest I used to do a little boxing, so I like to keep in shape...
As a matter of fact, just the other day I beat the living hell out of one of my parishioners.
Back off Padre, I'm Methodist.

RED MEAT
death takes a number
from the secret files of
max cannon
A couple years back I worked for this toy company that made these battery-operated toy dogs that could walk around and sit up and bark and stuff like that.
I lost that job 'cause the factory burned down and they didn't have no insurance. Anyways, the other night I'm watchin' the home shopping channel and they're sellin' those same dogs. So I'm wondering where'd they get 'em, since everything got burned up.
But then I remembered...them dogs were made out of asbestos.

RED MEAT
cute antidote
from the secret files of
max cannon
Honey...are you asleep? Sweetheart?
Huh...Ted, why are you up in the middle of the night?
Darling, do you love me...no matter what?
Yes of course I do, Ted. Now come back to bed.
Hey!! The bed is all wet! Damn! I can't believe you wet the bed!
But you still love me, right?

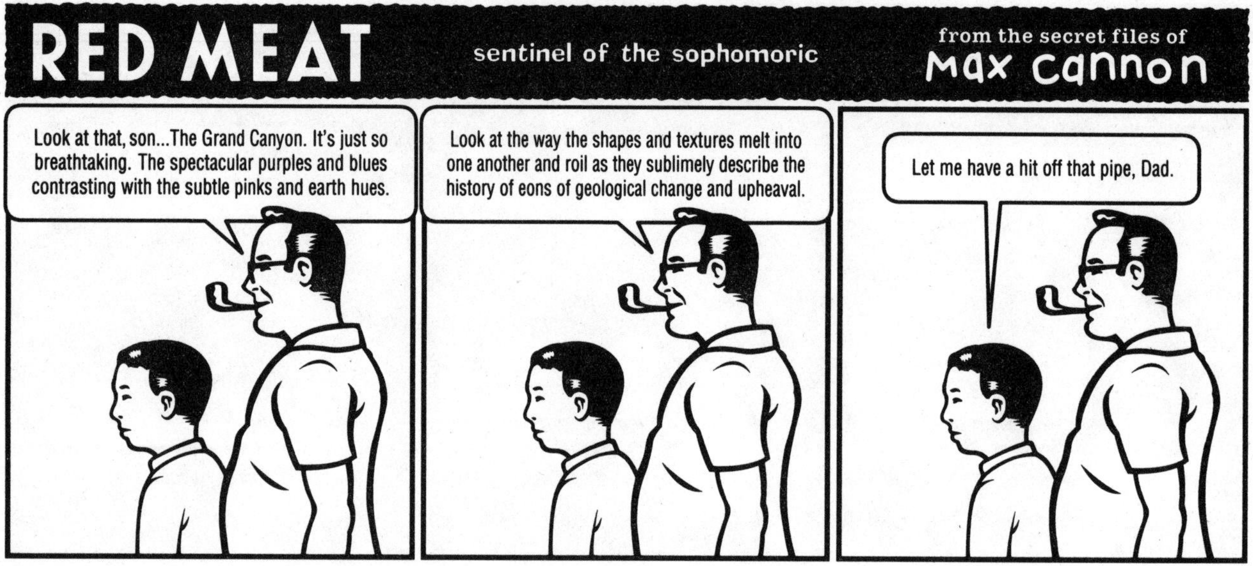
RED MEAT
sentinel of the sophomoric
from the secret files of
Max Cannon
Look at that, son...The Grand Canyon. It's just so breathtaking. The spectacular purples and blues contrasting with the subtle pinks and earth hues.
Look at the way the shapes and textures melt into one another and roil as they sublimely describe the history of eons of geological change and upheaval.
Let me have a hit off that pipe, Dad.

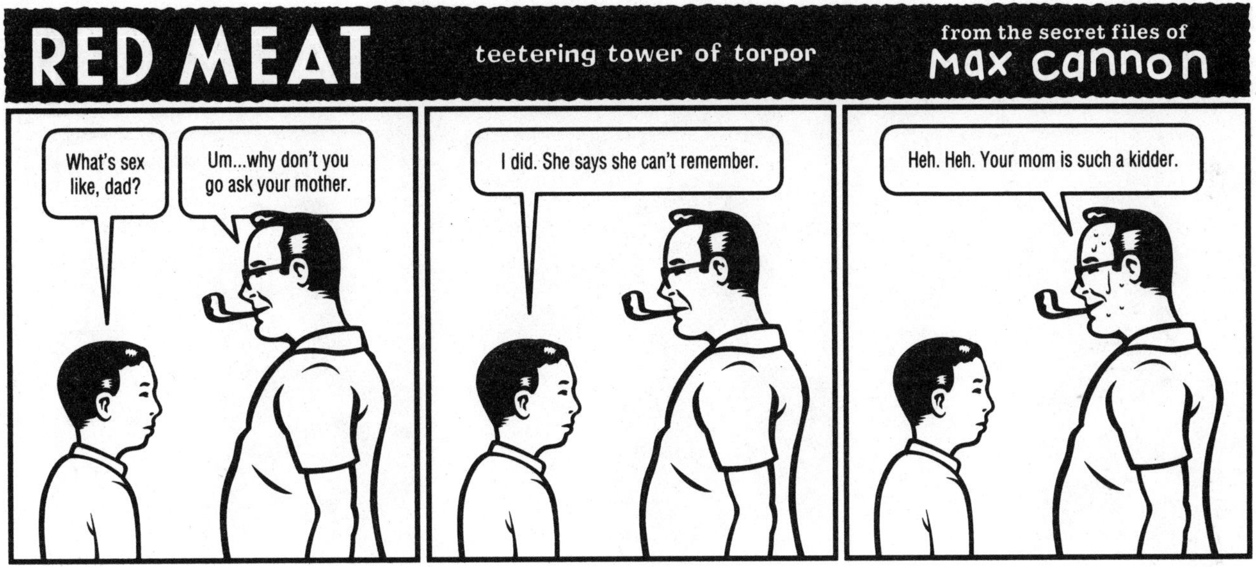
RED MEAT
teetering tower of torpor
from the secret files of
Max Cannon
What's sex like, dad?
Um...why don't you go ask your mother.
I did. She says she can't remember.
Heh. Heh. Your mom is such a kidder.

RED MEAT
pistol chicks in a machine gun nest
from the secret files of
max cannon
Cut myself shaving this morning.
Got pretty scratched up shaving the cat, too.

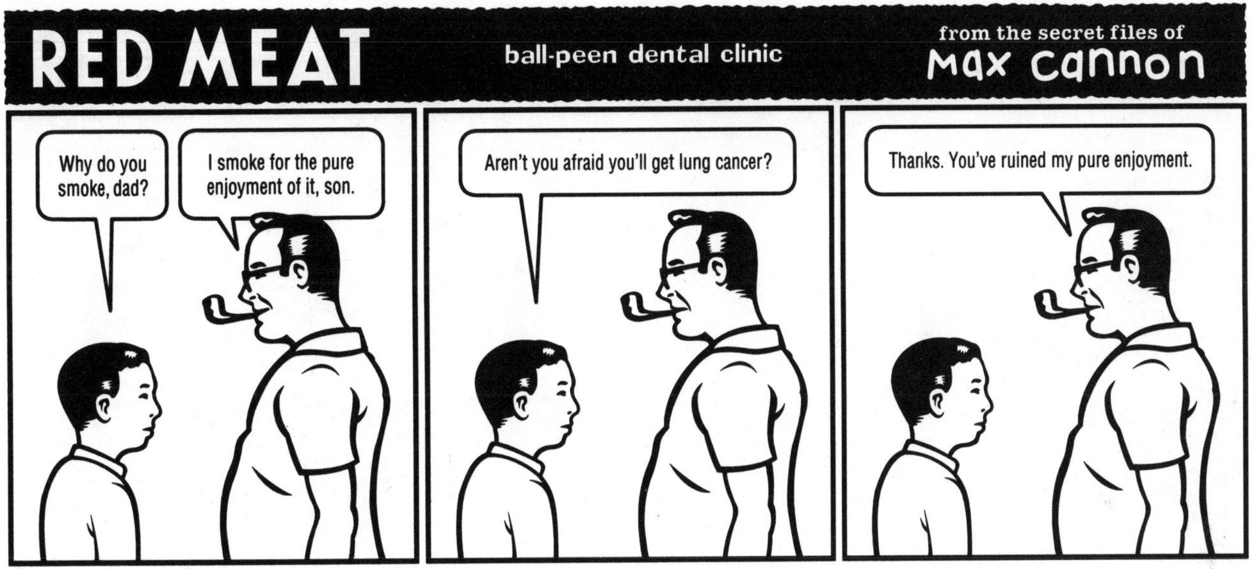
RED MEAT
ball-peen dental clinic
from the secret files of
max cannon
Why do you smoke, dad?
I smoke for the pure enjoyment of it, son.
Aren't you afraid you'll get lung cancer?
Thanks. You've ruined my pure enjoyment.

RED MEAT
this special comic strip
drawn by billy, age 8
from the secret files of
max cannon
WeL, son
how do you
Like your new
FiSShiNg rod?
Its
grate
dad.
oh no.
I have puLed
out My eyeBaLL
wiTh The
hook.
I think you
wiLL have beter
Luck iF you use
a worm.
EYEBALL

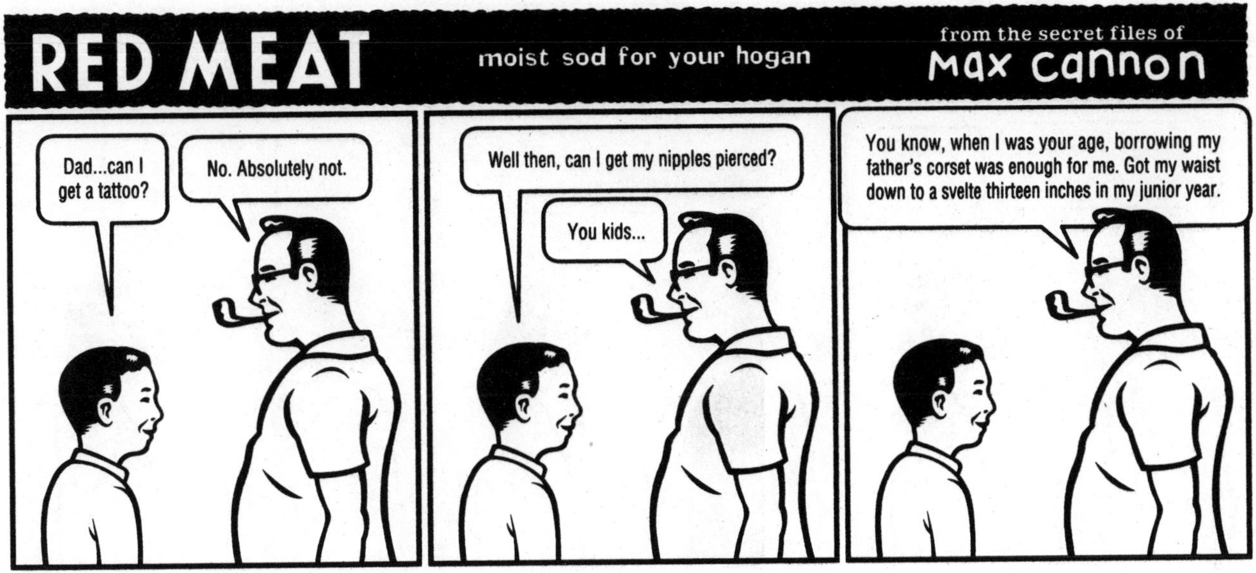
RED MEAT
moist sod for your hogan
from the secret files of
max cannon
Dad...can I get a tattoo?
No. Absolutely not.
Well then, can I get my nipples pierced?
You kids...
You know, when I was your age, borrowing my father's corset was enough for me. Got my waist down to a svelte thirteen inches in my junior year.

RED MEAT
more fun than a mouthful of live crickets
from the secret files of
max cannon
Morning, Ted. What are you doing up so early?
Watering the yard.
You are, of course, aware that you aren't wearing any pants?
Well Dan, it is, of course, my yard.

RED MEAT
busfare to nowhere
from the secret files of
max cannon
Say, are you a police officer?
Nope. Sorry. I'm just a milkman.
Oh.
Then you probably don't care that I just saw a guy get killed?
Not really. Did it involve milk?

RED MEAT
little foil balls for your fillings
from the secret files of
Max cannon
I was bowling with my girlfriend last night, and of course I whooped her. So she says, "does that make you feel like a big man...to beat a girl at bowling?
"Yes it does," I says...
"Yes it does."

RED MEAT
a big crunchy bowl of earwigs
from the secret files of
Max Cannon
Say, Dan...have you seen my son?
Yes, I have.
And he's no beauty contest winner, that's for sure.
What I meant was, have you seen him around?

RED MEAT
comedy that almost might have been
from the secret files of
Max Cannon
The other day I beat the daylights outta some guy.
And I'm pretty sure it was for no reason at all.

RED MEAT
pre-chewed for extra softness
from the secret files of
max cannon
Ahhh, there's nothing better than a nice, long, hot shower.
EEUULGH
Just don't drink the shampoo... no matter how good it smells.

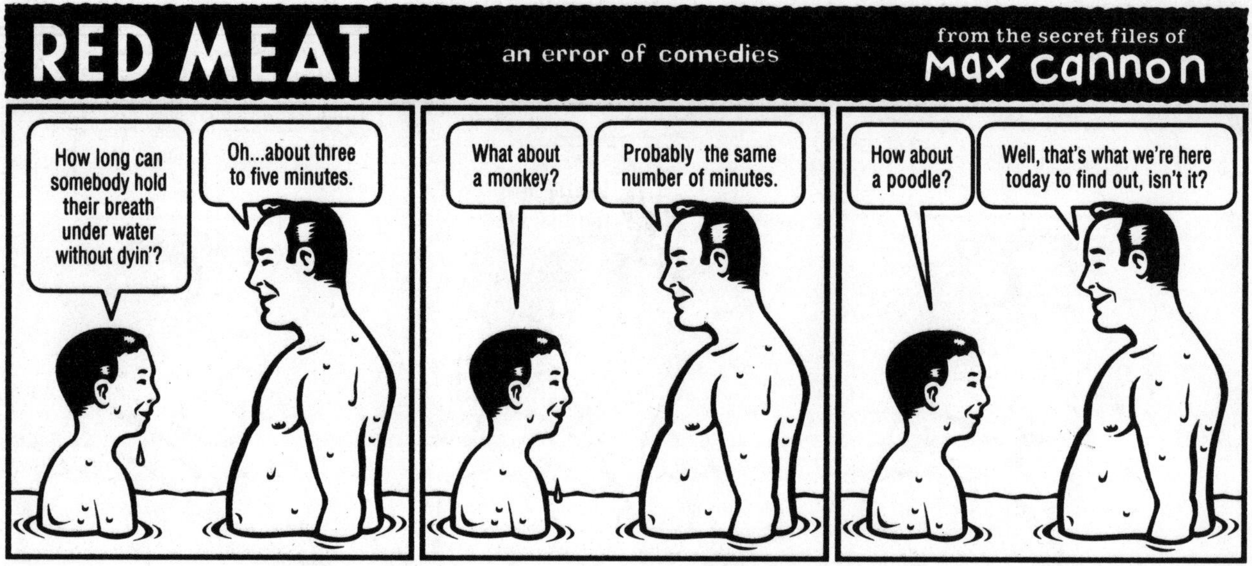
RED MEAT
an error of comedies
from the secret files of
Max Cannon
How long can somebody hold their breath under water without dyin'?
Oh...about three to five minutes.
What about a monkey?
Probably the same number of minutes.
How about a poodle?
Well, that's what we're here today to find out, isn't it?

RED MEAT
rotting teeth and soap-flavored candy
from the secret files of
Max Cannon
Mom always used to say: If life gives you poop...
Make poop-juice.

RED MEAT
spicy cajun-style pabulum
from the secret files of
max cannon
Honey...come look at the scale. I've lost a lot of weight this week.
Ted, you know full well that broken old scale always weighs everthing twenty pounds light.
And please take off that ridiculous-looking corset.
But sweetheart, it's the "William Shatner look."

RED MEAT
from the land of the big wee-wee
from the secret files of
max cannon
Whatcha gonna do with the gun, dad?
I'm going hunting.
Can I go with you?
No, I'm afraid not. It's too dangerous.
Besides, you don't know the first thing about tracking or field-dressing a poodle.
Oh.

RED MEAT
it's not just awful...it's god-awful
from the secret files of
Max Cannon
Mom, can I get braces?
Now, why would you want braces when you have such beautiful, straight teeth?
No...I meant for my legs.
Please get back under the porch before one of the neighbors sees you.

RED MEAT
shut up and pretend it's funny
from the secret files of
Max Cannon
My landlady was sick this morning, and I couldn't remember whether you're s'posed to feed a fever and starve a cold, or if it's the other way around.
I know one thing for sure, though...
You can't drown a cold.

RED MEAT
a nickel in the steaming grate of doom
from the secret files of
Max Cannon
Here's a good one. What do you call a guy who's slathered with thick mucous and singing "The Lady is a Tramp"?
I don't know...what?
"Frank Snotra." Get it? SNOT-tra.
Oh, that's a good one.
Much funnier than the poop joke, Lord.

RED MEAT
live bait in your underwear
from the secret files of
max cannon
Say, Dan...I know it's only seven in the morning, but why don't you come inside and have a drink.
I'd love to, Ted.
Dan
But I'm already drunk.
So am I.
Dan
Ha! Ha! Ha! Ha! Ha! Ha!
Dan

RED MEAT
the information frontage road
from the secret files of
max cannon
I had this queer dream last night.
My head wuz normal, but my body turned into a pine cone and it wuz bein' eaten by giant squirrels.
Giant lady squirrels.

RED MEAT
a comic strip this insipid should at least come with a piece of bubble gum
from the secret files of
max cannon
Tell me the truth...if robbers came up to your truck with guns, and told you they were gonna shoot you if you didn't give them all the milk, what would you do?
Why...I'd whip a nerve gas ampule out of my utility belt and they'd die writhing in agony.
That's a big lie! You don't even have any dumb old utility belt!
Hah! Hah! I guess you've called my bluff, little lady. Actually, I'd probably grab a little child like you, for example, and try to use it as a human shield.
I hope you die and get ate by worms, Milkman Dan.

RED MEAT
wide-open crap spigot
from the secret files of
max cannon
Hiya Ted. Need any gag and novelty supplies today? They're guaranteed to be 100% funny.
Gee Vern, I don't know if I should...
That exploding gum you sold me burned the inside of my wife's mouth pretty bad. She had to get seven stitches in her lip as well.
Oh my.
So...was it funny?

RED MEAT
a picture is worth a thousand welts
from the secret files of
Max Cannon
Mom! I'm gonna borrow your mop handle for awhile...okay?
What for?
Me and the guys are gonna play "penitentiary."
So...you're the guard, and that's your shotgun?
No. I'm a bald-headed inmate named Debbie, and this is supposed to really be a mop handle.
Please be careful.

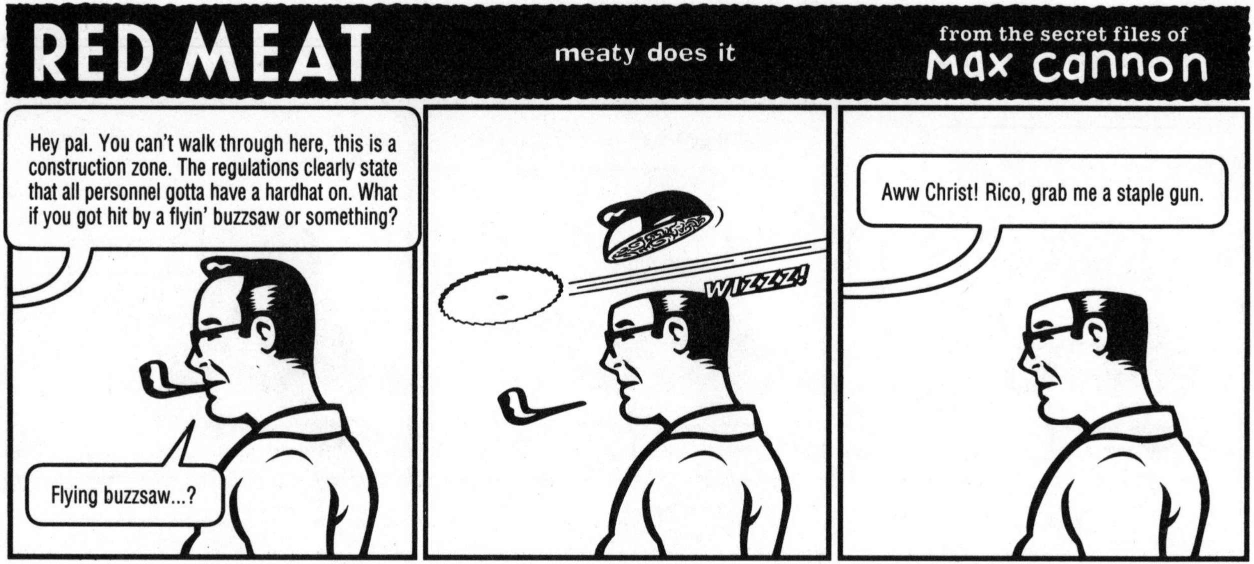
RED MEAT
meaty does it
from the secret files of
max cannon
Hey pal. You can't walk through here, this is a construction zone. The regulations clearly state that all personnel gotta have a hardhat on. What if you got hit by a flyin' buzzsaw or something?
Flying buzzsaw...?
WIZZZ!
Aww Christ! Rico, grab me a staple gun.

RED MEAT
now more chocolatey than ever
from the secret files of
max cannon
Some day I wish they would do a movie about my life. And it would all be true...
Except for the one part where I rescue the underwear girls from the volcano.

RED MEAT
the devil's puppet show
from the secret files of
Max Cannon
Hmm...perhaps I've been a bit harsh with the neighborhood kids. Possibly, they're a bit too young to enjoy my particular brand of humor.
It is conceivable that what I regard as innocent jibes are, in reality, traumatizing episodes to their innocent young minds.
Jeez...that's the booze talking.

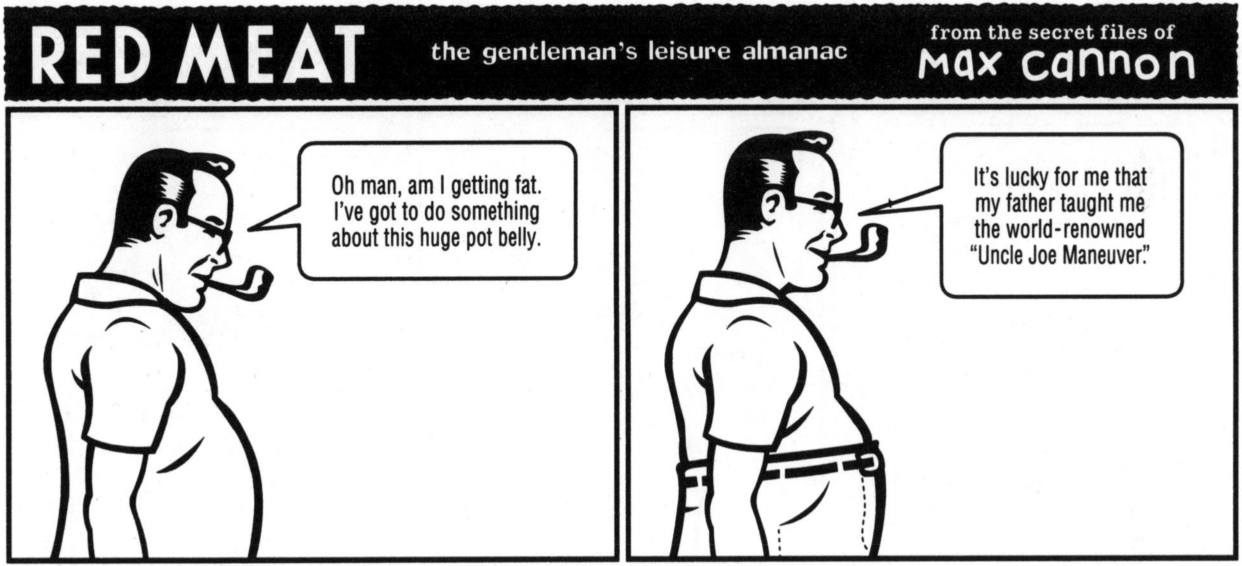
RED MEAT
the gentleman's leisure almanac
from the secret files of
Max Cannon
Oh man, am I getting fat. I've got to do something about this huge pot belly.
It's lucky for me that my father taught me the world-renowned "Uncle Joe Maneuver."

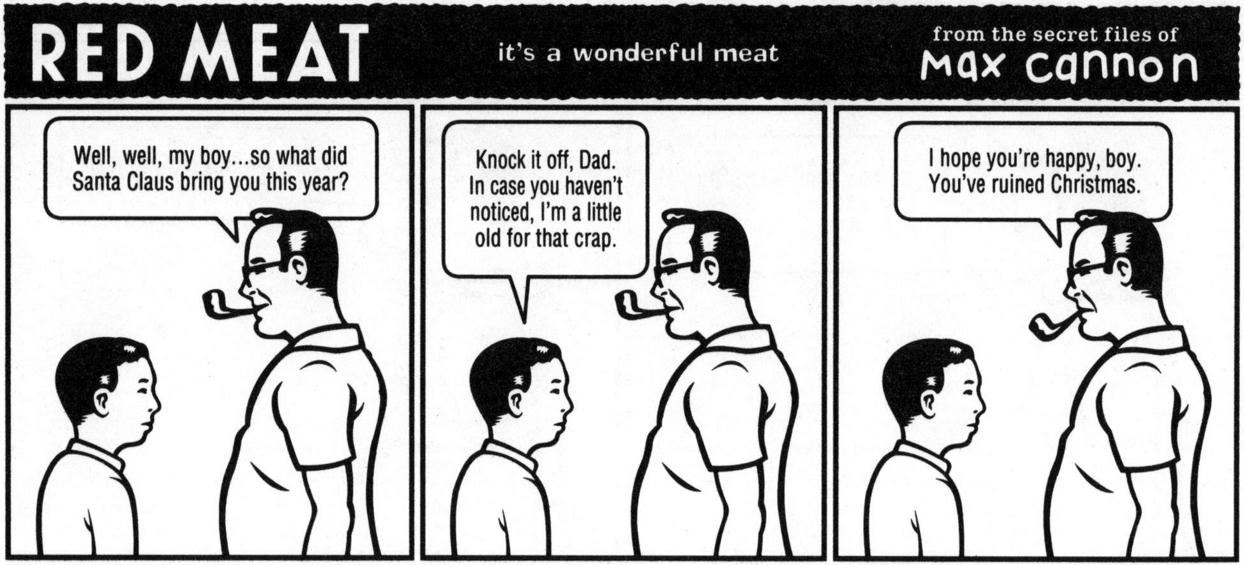
RED MEAT
it's a wonderful meat
from the secret files of
max cannon
Well, well, my boy...so what did Santa Claus bring you this year?
Knock it off, Dad. In case you haven't noticed, I'm a little old for that crap.
I hope you're happy, boy. You've ruined Christmas.

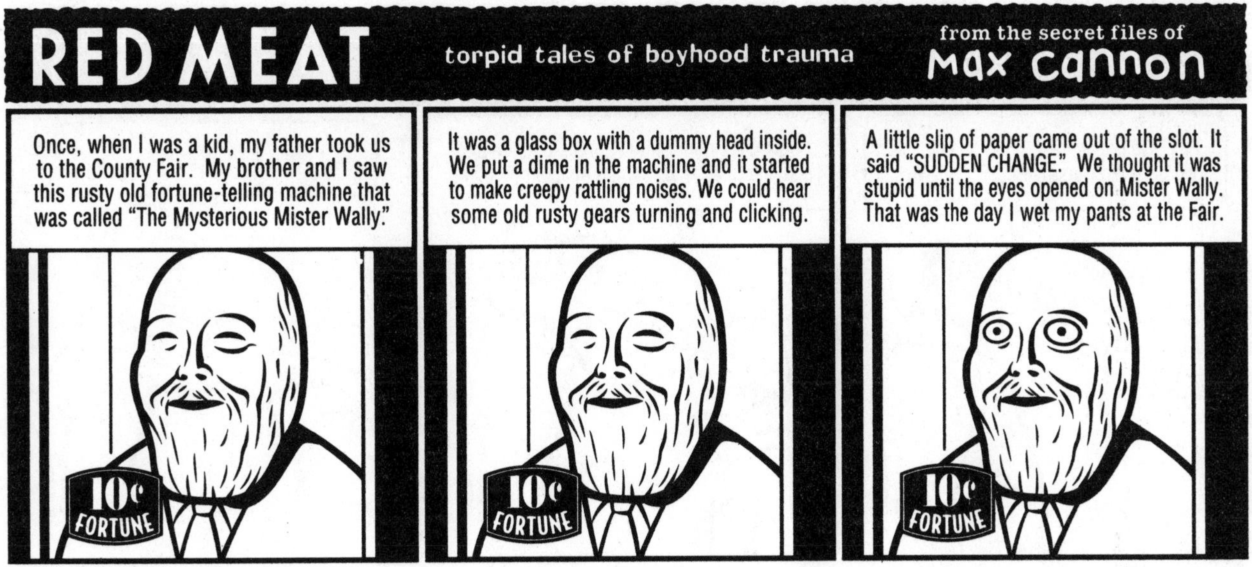
RED MEAT
torpid tales of boyhood trauma
from the secret files of
max cannon
Once, when I was a kid, my father took us to the County Fair. My brother and I saw this rusty old fortune-telling machine that was called "The Mysterious Mister Wally."
10¢
FORTUNE
It was a glass box with a dummy head inside. We put a dime in the machine and it started to make creepy rattling noises. We could hear some old rusty gears turning and clicking.
10¢
FORTUNE
A little slip of paper came out of the slot. It said "SUDDEN CHANGE." We thought it was stupid until the eyes opened on Mister Wally. That was the day I wet my pants at the Fair.
10¢
FORTUNE

RED MEAT
industrial strength comedy remover
from the secret files of
Max Cannon
Hey, I've got an idea. What do you say we go build ourselves a snow man?
Geez, Dad... I don't know.
I mean, it's about fifty degrees outside and raining...maybe we should build a rain man.
By God, you're as drunk as I am.

RED MEAT
groundhog day massacre
from the secret files of
max cannon
Oh boy...I just screwed the pooch.
Rarf
Excuse me. I meant to say "made love."

RED MEAT
comedy that's with the angels now
from the secret files of
Max Cannon
Ted, Sweetheart...why are you walking around naked with a gun in your hand?
Can't talk now, honey-cakes...
I'm on nude patrol.

RED MEAT
eating spider egg sacs like capers
from the secret files of
max cannon
I got kicked out of a funeral today.
Jeez...I was only tryin' to see if them eyes were sewed shut.

RED MEAT
love nuggets for snuggle-butts
from the secret files of
max cannon
Honey, I thought I'd wear something special to bed tonight. It's a latex, uh...marital aid.
Good God, Ted. It makes you look like a big, black, shiny rubber yam.
A big, black, shiny rubber "love yam."

RED MEAT
ill-fitting underclamp
from the secret files of
max cannon
Dad, are you gonna keep wearing that rubber bondage suit forever?
Because, if you are...I'm running away.
What's the matter? Can't handle being the son of the "Lloyd Bridges of love?"

RED MEAT
the frosting on the fatback
from the secret files of
max cannon
Hiya, Ted.
What can I
do you for?
Hi Wally, I need a small
can of mild Cavendish.
tobacco shack
Coming right up. Say...how'd you like that
"Philosopher's Blend" I sold you last week?
tobacco shack
I'm still coming down off it, man.
Right on.
tobacco shack

RED MEAT
suddenly...the sidewalk
from the secret files of
Max Cannon
Y'know Wally, this pipe's finish has lost its luster. Do you sell pipe wax or something?
Not really...
tobacco shack
What I generally use is a good-sized shot of mucus rubbed into a moist chamois cloth. Would you like me to shine her up for you?
No thanks.
tobacco shack
Kids these days...I'm glad I didn't tell him about how to remoisturize stale tobacco with a fresh cat stool.
tobacco shack

RED MEAT
kiss the vibrating chihuahua
from the secret files of
Max Cannon
When I was a kid, I usedta be real shy around people. My mother told me to imagine them in their underwear, so they wouldn't be so scary.
I still have nightmares about them scary underwear people.

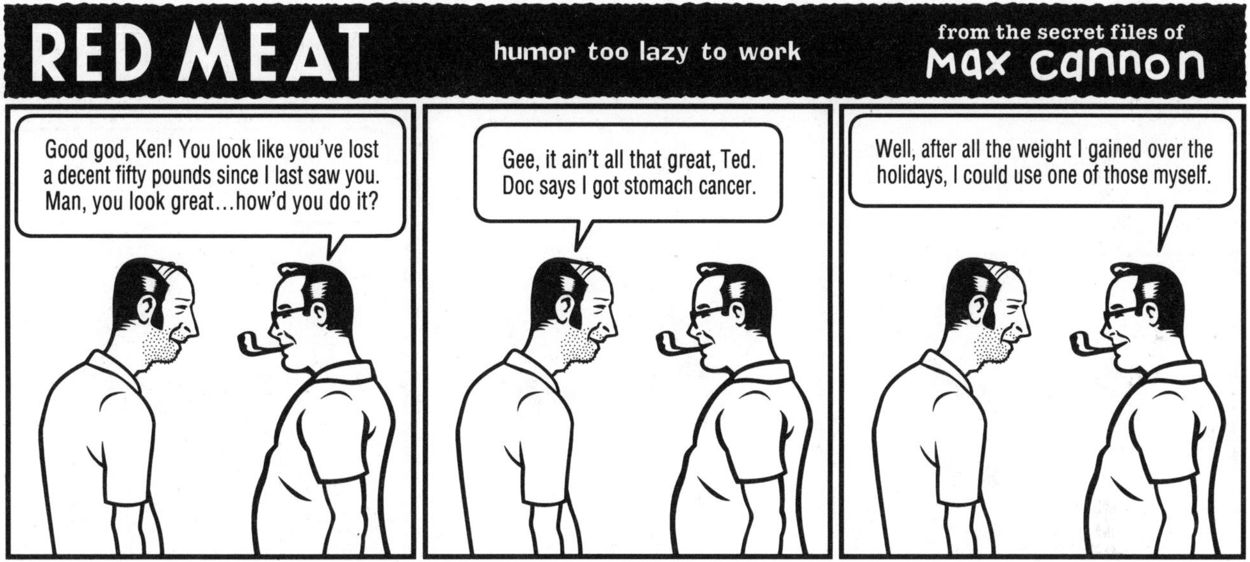
RED MEAT
humor too lazy to work
from the secret files of
Max Cannon
Good god, Ken! You look like you've lost a decent fifty pounds since I last saw you. Man, you look great...how'd you do it?
Gee, it ain't all that great, Ted. Doc says I got stomach cancer.
Well, after all the weight I gained over the holidays, I could use one of those myself.

RED MEAT
the wet carpet treatment
from the secret files of
max cannon
Jeez. The other day it was really hot. I guess I must've had heat stroke because I got real woozy and threw up, so I decided I better take off my clothes and lay down for a little while.
It didn't help, though...the bus driver made me get out at the very next stop.

RED MEAT
the broccoli in your windpipe
from the secret files of
max cannon
Mom? Can I borrow some quarters out of your purse?
What for?
I'm gonna use 'em to hold Larry's eyes open
I don't think it's a good idea for you to stick things in your friend's eyes.
But Mom, he fell out of the tree and he's not breathin'.
Well, alright... you can have two quarters.

RED MEAT
those aren't raisins
from the secret files of
max cannon
Psst! Hey, Dad?
Shhh. The movie is starting now.
Dad...can I please have some candy?
Here. Here you go. Now try to be quiet, okay?
Okay.
This is gross, Dad. It doesn't even taste like candy. What kind is it, anyways?
I don't know. It was stuck to the bottom of my seat.

RED MEAT
rhubarb in your coal shute
from the secret files of
max cannon
Enjoying the movie, son?
Not really. It's kind of dumb.
I don't know, I kind of like it.
Yeah Dad, but you're drunk.
Hey, you had your chance in the car, Mister "I only drink name-brand gin."

RED MEAT
third-degree indian burn
from the secret files of
max cannon
My hamster had five babies last week. This morning when I looked in the cage, she had ate two of them little babies.
What the heck. Had a couple myself.

RED MEAT
eating shoe leather like jerky
from the secret files of
max cannon
Well Karen, today is the last day for home milk delivery. I guess the Milkman has gone the way of the paperboy. We're both an extinct species. Don't worry though...
Dan
I've already taken a new job driving the ice cream truck in this same neighborhood.
Hey! What happened to the nice old man who usually drives the ice cream truck?
Dan
Maybe he was visited one night by the "ghost of ice cream past," and maybe that ghost was a little too scary for an old man with a serious heart condition. Maybe that ghost is sorry now.
There was a scary ghost outside my window last week.
Yes, I know.
Dan

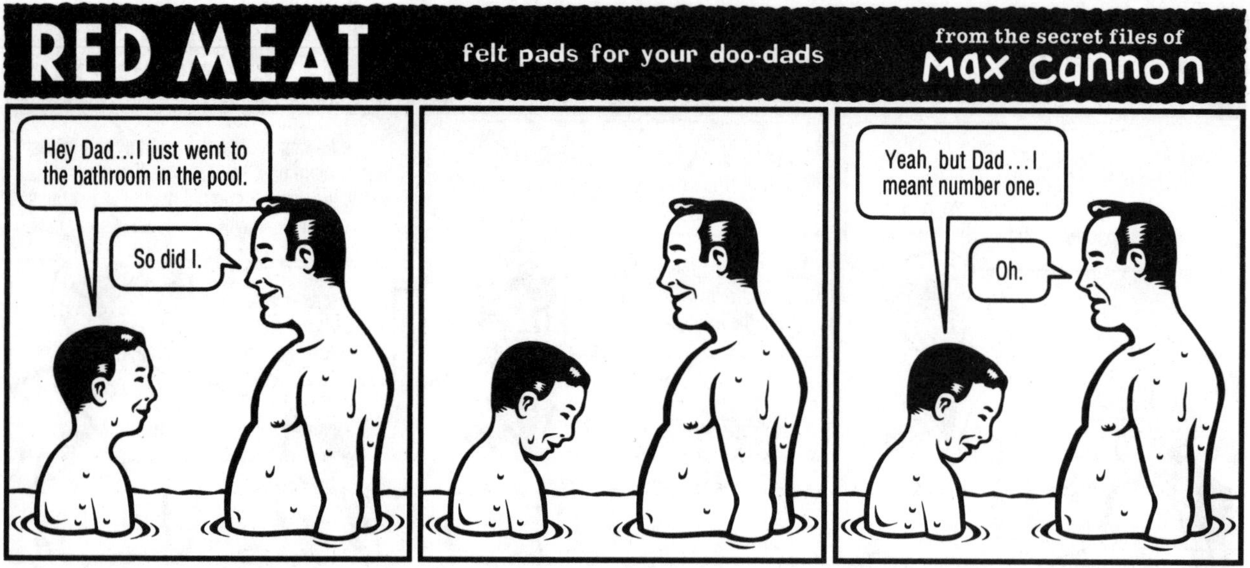
RED MEAT
felt pads for your doo-dads
from the secret files of
Max Cannon
Hey Dad...I just went to the bathroom in the pool.
So did I.
Yeah, but Dad...I meant number one.
Oh.

RED MEAT
flaccid ends, sagging middle
from the secret files of
max cannon
I got kicked out of the grocery store today.
I asked the stock lady where I could find the "ladies' needs section," and she asks "what kind of ladies' needs?"
So I says "inflatable ladies' needs." Then she calls the manager to make me leave.

RED MEAT
makes up in flavor what it lacks in taste
from the secret files of max cannon
Hey, little lady. How'd you like a nice big piece of chocolate candy?
Go away, dumbo-head.
Dan
Hey...is that any way to talk to your old pal, Milkman Dan?
The last time you gave me candy, it tasted yucky and I got sick and throwed up!
Dan
Whoa! So that's what happened to those prescription antihistamines. Here's a little safety tip, Karen: don't take candy from adults when they're really, really drunk.
I hate you, Milkman Dan.
Dan

RED MEAT
pocket-size bile geyser
from the secret files of
max cannon
My girlfriend says to me: "stop pickin' at that scab, Earl, or it's never gonna heal."
What the heck...
It's her lip.

RED MEAT
the comic for tomato soup-skin eaters
from the secret files of
Max Cannon
Ted, sweetheart...somebody's left a wicker basket with a little baby in it on our front doorstep. There's even a little note attached.
I'll be darned. What's it say?
It says: "Please take care of my precious little angel. He was born with a rare and incurable medical condition, and I am not able to pay the hundreds of thousands of dollars to give him the treatment he needs."
Oh Ted…what should we do?
Just leave it out there on the stoop, honey. The cats'll get it.

RED MEAT
new uses for the same old juices
from the secret files of
Max Cannon
Ted! There's a bird in the laundry room. It must have flown in when I was taking the laundry out to the clothesline. I hate birds!
I know, honey. I'll get rid of it.
Oh god! It's flying around all over the place! Hurry, please!
I'm coming... just hang on.
What do you need that for? It's just a teensy little bird.
You're right, dear. I'd better go get my staple gun.

RED MEAT
the comic strip that revitalized the refrigerator magnet industry
from the secret files of
max cannon
Hey Ted, thanks for lending me "All Man." I read the whole book last night, and it's really put me in touch with my true inner "Brute Force." It changed my life overnight.
That's fantastic, Reuben. Y'know, the chapter by Charlton Heston really helped me to admit that I've always liked swimsuit calendars, and that I never wanted to be "a sensitive male."
Hey, you wanna go find a parking lot and beat the the hell out of some total stranger?
Chill out, Spartacus.

RED MEAT
half-inch wig staple
from the secret files of
max cannon
Say there, kids...what are you two so intent on over there?
I'm teaching Simon how to count to six.
Six! Six!
That's good, but why don't you teach him how to count to ten instead?
But Dad...a grasshopper's only got six legs that you can pick off for counting.
Then you boys hold on and I'll go get the cat. We're going to learn to count to ten, by god.
You rule, Dad!
Yaaaay!

RED MEAT
death rattle from a gallstone maraca
from the secret files of
max cannon
A couple years ago I wrote a story based on that movie "Old Yeller." Except in my version Old Yeller don't get shot when he gets rabies.
Instead, he goes crazy and steals a police car and then goes on an interstate killing spree.
That way you don't get as sad when the Green Berets electrocute him.

RED MEAT
sermon-free humor
from the secret files of
max cannon
Well Dan, I've considered it very carefully and I'm left with no choice but to fire you or change your morning milk delivery route.
Why's that boss?
Dan
Let's see...I've got two complaints of verbal abuse by you, one for property damage, four complaints of sexual harrassment, setting a fire to someone's cat, and public drunkeness.
I'm sorry sir...
Dan
I was only trying to establish a strong "dairy presence" in the neighborhood.
Dan

RED MEAT
locust leavings on the loaf of levity
from the secret files of
max cannon
My goodness, look at all the birds on that telephone wire.
Those are clothes pins on a clothesline, Dad.
Wow. These are definitely the strongest non-prescription cough drops available.
I could use another one.

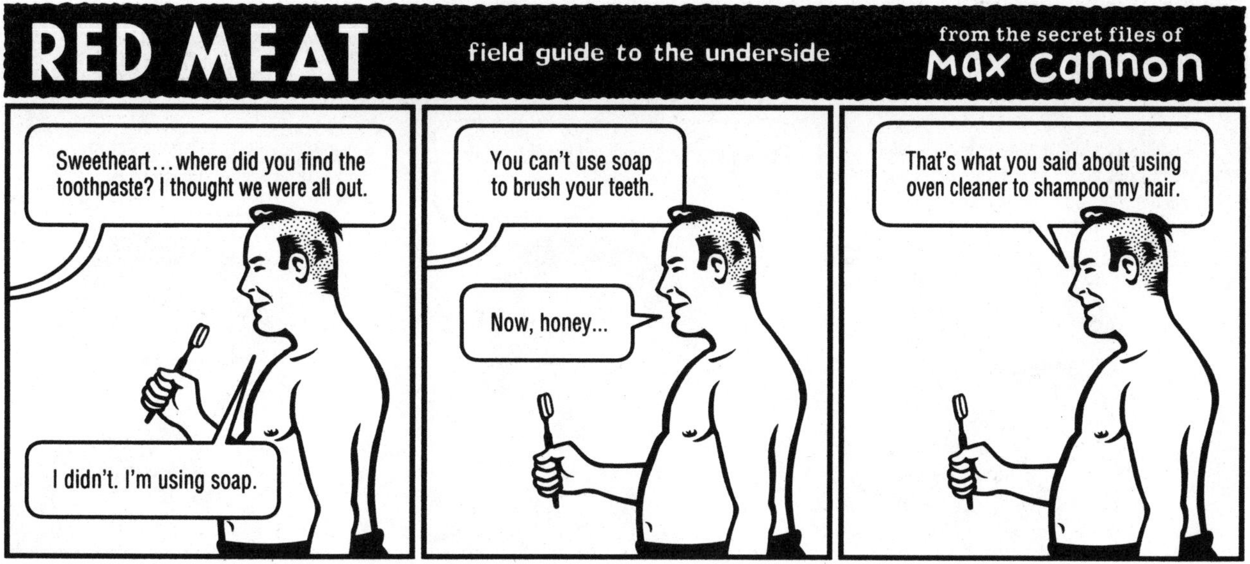
RED MEAT
field guide to the underside
from the secret files of
Max Cannon
Sweetheart...where did you find the toothpaste? I thought we were all out.
I didn't. I'm using soap.
You can't use soap to brush your teeth.
Now, honey...
That's what you said about using oven cleaner to shampoo my hair.

RED MEAT
underdone overkill aftermath
from the secret files of
Max Cannon
Last night I was lookin' out my window, and I notice this guy lookin' at me from the building across the way. So I take off my clothes and do a nekkid dance to make him quit lookin.'
When I look back, he has his clothes off, and he's doin' a little nekkid dance also.
Pretty good dancer, too.

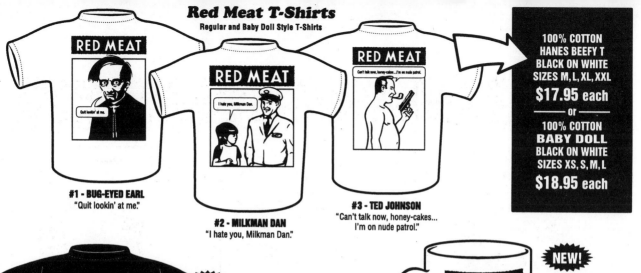

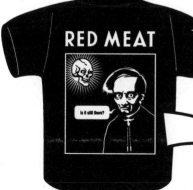

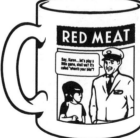